Eyes

# Sergei's Eyes

## REFLECTIONS OF SOUL LESSONS

BY

Karen Fullerton

*Sergei's Eyes: Reflections of Soul Lessons*
ISBN: 978-0-692-80191-8
Copyright © 2016 by Karen Fullerton

Cover design: Kate Rader
Cover concept: Karen Fullerton
Cover photos: Sergei's eyes, Laura Pope; Sergei in woods, Graham Fullerton; Sergei's ashes, Phillip Fullerton; Author photo, Tracy Krell.

*But then again it feels like some sort of inspiration*
*To let the next life off the hook*
*Or she'll say look what I had to overcome from*
*my last life*
*I think I'll write a book*

*How long 'til my soul gets it right*
*Can any human being ever reach the highest light*
*Except for Galileo, God rest his soul*
*King of night vision, King of insight*

Galileo Lyrics (partial)
Indigo Girls

# To Sergei,

*my rock, who continues to be my inspiration from the
other side in helping people and their pets.*

*Also to my pets Samantha, Sydney, Jude and Jade:
My princess, my protector, my funny man, and my love
bug. Thank you for your healing and inspiration
in so many other ways.*

# Contents

# PREFACE

## "Me too."

When someone says, "Me too!" in response to a belief you have or to a similar situation as yours, don't you feel a bit lighter? Your heart feels a little warmer because there's someone else who truly can relate to what you are going through. Even if it's a stranger you talk to in a coffee shop who you will never see again, you are forever changed, even if just a tiny bit, because you can release some of the weight you've been holding on to. It's not "just you" this has happened to.

When we have the courage to share our personal experiences and someone understands and connects with us, healing has occurred.

It doesn't matter what the belief or issue is that you are going through. It could be that you don't seem to make friends easily, or you went through a painful divorce, or you constantly are finding yourself in the wrong job.

Maybe you lost a son or daughter early in life. Perhaps you have different beliefs or ideals from your family. It doesn't matter. There is no measuring system that says what we are going through is any less significant than someone else's experience. Pain is pain. Joy is joy. What matters is that someone else has been there, done that, and has lived a similar path as you. They get it. They say, "Me too." It's at that realization point that you don't feel quite as alone anymore. You are connected!

The "me too" concept is not new, but it's powerful. I heard it from the rector at my church during one of his sermons, and it finally clicked for me why I was to write this book. For over five years I had wanted to write a book but could never figure out how stories about my dog would interest anyone else. Would it be a novel or memoir? What would the plot be? Could my experiences be of help to other people? Like most of us, I was good at self-doubt and second-guessing myself. So many others have faced greater hardships than me; who was I to think that my pain or learning experiences were worth publishing? I just couldn't connect the dots on purpose of my book. That is, until that one fateful Sunday. Then it clicked! My stories, simple as they may be, could be someone else's "me too" moment.

These moments are what connect us to other people and allow us to truly be compassionate. I know I'm not the only one who has learned lessons from their dog.

Our pets are our teachers. One of their greatest gifts is to guide us in self-reflection. My insight to the lessons and teachings from my dog, Sergei, came after his passing. Reflecting on memorable events during our time together has given me a greater understanding of his importance in my life, raising his significance to a completely different level. What were simple life events turned into life and soul lessons.

Sergei's eyes were always his primary feature. Everyone always commented how beautiful they were—so blue, clear, and kind. Many said they felt like Sergei's eyes could see into their soul. Like Paulo Coelho said, "The eyes are the mirror of the soul and reflect everything that seems to be hidden; and like a mirror, they also reflect the person looking into them." Those eyes definitely saw into mine.

It's my wish that these stories will resonate with you, making a difference in your life by inspiring your own self-reflection and desire to connect and share with others. I'm sure there is someone else who needs to hear what *you* have to say, as well. We all need to know we are not alone. I hope you enjoy at least one "me too" moment through my soul lessons reflected in *Sergei's Eyes*.

*Karen Fullerton*

# THE BEGINNING

# I am...

I was a child of divorced parents and lived as a latch-key kid when it wasn't as taboo to admit that. My family moved to Brighton, Michigan when I was in the fourth grade, and we lived on a lake. Our house was surrounded by beautiful, tall, old trees that I admired; they made me feel safe. I didn't have many friends so I daydreamed a lot and played with our family dog, Heidi, who was my best friend until she died when I was 11 years old. From my childhood, I learned how to be independent, but what I really wanted more than anything was to be accepted and to connect with people.

My grandma was an important person in my life. While I was still young, she developed diabetes and also had a heart attack. Over the next several years, she was in and out of the hospital often, and that's when I thought I wanted to become a nurse when I grew up. I walked down the hospital halls imagining that I was working there, going to help people get better. At home, I took care of Grandma a lot, organizing her pills and being her care-giver of sorts when I was just a pre-teen.

Of all my childhood memories, these items stick out most as they play an ever-important role in my life now. As an adult, I am a healer, but not in the form of a nurse. I obtained my Reiki Master/Teacher designation in 2001, primarily because of my desire to heal the earth, animals, and others. So often what matters in childhood becomes a big part of our life as we age. It certainly has for me. Through the legacy of my Siberian Husky, Sergei, and the foundation that bears his name, I am able to help and heal hundreds of people and their pets.

In order to get here, I had to connect the dots first. It was not a quick transition. It took about twenty years. Let me tell you, I'm an impatient person, so if your heart just sank when you read how long it could take to put the puzzle pieces of life together, don't worry; your path will unfold in your own time. I had many lessons to learn first, and I'm still learning. We always are.

I started off on the traditional path, attended college and studied business in undergrad. I advanced in the corporate world in various marketing positions and developed strategic planning skills which led me to be a marketing consultant and graphic designer. After fifteen years of spending no more than two to three years in any one job because of discontent and inner boredom, I was drawn to go back to school and obtain my MBA. In 2010 I graduated top in my class with a 4.0 GPA and was invited by the president of the university to speak at my commencement ceremony. I thought that was it—that I had arrived! I pictured a promotion, a six-figure income, and final happiness. Nope. Well, it was a step moving me toward final happiness, just not in the timing or as a result of financial means the way I had originally thought.

I have now arrived at happiness in my life, but not without some painful experiences. I had no idea how important these life experiences would be in bridging my life, connecting my past to my ultimate passion and spiritual purpose.

So who am I? A frightened little blonde-haired girl looking for acceptance, who grew into a young woman fearing abandonment, who became an impatient woman trying to create my happiness instead of letting it just happen. Now, I am a healer and a teacher, yet always a student. I married a bit later in life, at age 38, to a man who is truly my partner and best friend, who lets me be my strong, independent self. We are "parents" to our pets, as our plan for children was not in the overall universal plan. Most of all, I am happy.

We are always students continually learning for as long as we are breathing on this planet. I don't claim to know it all, by any means, and I personally do not respond to preaching or people telling me what to do. What I do like are stories—parables that you can apply to your own life, or not, as they fit. It is my wish that some of my stories connect with you.

# The guest

I grew up with a dog. Heidi was a beautiful German Shepherd and a huge part of my life. My mom used to tell me that when I took naps as a young child, I would rest my head on Heidi's belly, and she would not move until I woke up. I didn't realize how much I loved that dog until later in life. When I see the projects I made in elementary school that my mom kept, Heidi is mentioned or drawn in almost all of them. She was part of my third grade coat of arms. My list of "likes and dislikes" had her at the top of the "like" column. When I was six-years-old, Heidi was the subject of my first photographs, even if she didn't quite make it completely in the picture!

Heidi was one of my only friends. As a child, I never really felt like I fit in. I had some friends at school, but at home it seemed like I was always being excluded from neighborhood clubhouses or playtime. Heidi was always my go-to—my pal who understood me. She passed away when I was in middle school, and our house was very quiet after she was gone.

It wasn't until I was an adult, age twenty-eight, that I decided I wanted a dog of my own. I had thought about it before, but the responsibility and cost of owning a pet wasn't something I was ready to take on before that point in my life. Maybe I still wasn't really ready, but it's all I thought about. I wanted companionship. My love life had been a string of failures or road blocks, and I was aching for unconditional love. The quest for a dog began!

I thought I wanted a Samoyed or a similar breed that was fluffy—I wanted a dog that would feel good when I hugged him. I also wanted a dog that I could immediately take rollerblading or to exercise with me, but I didn't want a puppy (or so I thought!) because of the added responsibilities of potty-training, teething issues, etc. So off I went to the local humane society to look at dogs that were at least one or two years old. I saw a tan German Shepherd puppy that was so cute! Of course, I reminisced about my childhood and my relationship with Heidi, but this puppy was too young at just a few months old. I left the humane society without filling out an application, as I really thought I would only get a dog that was out of puppyhood.

A few weeks passed. I didn't go looking again but still wanted a dog very badly. I had started dating an old boy-friend who now lived an hour away from me. We attended the Fourth of July fireworks show together, and the next morning I saw in bold print in the classified section of the newspaper, "Red and White Siberian Husky Puppies." I knew what a Siberian Husky looked like, but I wasn't sure what a red and white one meant. All I could think of was an Irish Setter! My curiosity got the best of me, and I just had to go see.

The location was on my direct route back home, so I stopped in to "just look" at what this color of puppy looked like. Oh my! I took one look at the two playfully-romping 10-week-old huskies with blue eyes, felt their soft fur, and my heart melted. The only decision was to select which of the two puppies I wanted. One was really outgoing and came right up to me while the other one hung back. I thought I wanted the friendly one. When I went back a couple hours later to pick him up, there was only one puppy left, the quieter one, the one I was not going to choose. I feel the universe stepped in and had the other puppy get adopted before I got back. This was the one I was supposed to have!

# The name

I wanted to name my new puppy something unique and that was fitting for him. Nothing against names like "Spot" or "Jack"—I just wanted something a little more personal. As I was driving, I pondered what to name him. I was ready to bring home my new family member, but what would I call him? I kept thinking of his coloring—red and white. Then his breed—Siberian Husky. What was a fitting name? Then on the radio there was a recap of the recent NFL Stanley Cup Play-offs. It was 1997, and the Detroit Red Wings had swept the playoffs with their first Stanley Cup win since 1955. I was a fan. I lived outside of Detroit and had been to many hockey games at Joe Lewis Arena. The announcer started talking, "... Sergei Federov, one of the Wings' Russian Five led the playoffs in scoring..." That's it! I knew that was it! As soon as I heard the name Sergei, I felt a warmth in my chest and my body almost tingled as if telling me this should be my puppy's name.

When I had collected this bundle of fur to take home with me ("Bubba" as he was originally called), I'd put him in the back of the car. The seats were laid down flat extending the trunk area. This way, he could walk on a flat surface (before I knew about doggie seat belts! Or were they even available then?). I asked him, "How would you like to be named Sergei? You are red and white, from Russia, and Sergei is definitely a unique, strong name."

Immediately, I felt this little nose nuzzle in between the back of my right shoulder blade and the seat. He just kept it there as if to signify a response for loving his new name. Normally, you have to train a puppy to recognize and respond to their name with positive reinforcement, stroking, and treats until they learn that responding to that word is a good thing. Not with Sergei. He literally knew his name from the moment I asked him about it. He immediately looked at me with those big, blue eyes as if to say, "Yes, that's my name."

# REFLECTIONS

# Reflections

*After I first brought Sergei home*, all he did was sleep for what seemed like a week straight. He didn't have that puppy-energy that I was expecting or was warned about. When I was still thinking of getting a dog, my mom would say things like, "they cost a lot of money with vet bills," and "puppies take so much work; it's like having a toddler in the house—you have to watch them constantly." After this first week I thought all of these things must have been a myth. This cute fur ball was no trouble at all!

Maybe Sergei had just been getting used to his new home because after day seven it was like Dr. Jekyll and Mr. Hyde. Well, maybe not that bad, but this calm puppy now just constantly wanted to play! Thank goodness he was not a barker, but he always wanted my attention, brought me toys to tug, or would incessantly squeak others. If I took my eye off of him, he'd wander about finding new items he thought *should* be his toys. At night he would whine in his crate, and the 6 a.m. workday would come far too soon. I wanted to prove to my mom that I could handle this responsibility. After all, she tried to prepare me! Then came potty training and the accidents in the home, although I have to admit, he did learn that very quickly. He was a ball of energy, and I didn't feel like I could take even one minute for myself. I was a single, 28-year-old who suddenly felt like my freedom was going to be gone forever.

I was so tired. I broke down and called my mom. "Do you want a puppy?" I asked her. I was half serious, waiting to hear what she said. If she had said yes, oh how the course of my life and others would be so different! I'm so glad she had that motherly wisdom. She didn't chide me or tell me the dreaded "I told you so," but rather she comforted me and told me I could do this. With the wisdom of a mother who raised four children, she told me "It gets easier. Just get through the moment and enjoy these times; they pass far too quickly, and then they're gone."

I am grateful to my mom for supporting me that day so that I kept Sergei. I didn't know then how important Sergei would be in my life or that he would be my greatest teacher. He was helping me learn life lessons, from the get-go before I even realized it, that could be applied to other areas of my life.

For instance, I had always worked hard for what I wanted. I had to pay for my own college education, so I saved from my job and kept good grades in order to get a scholarship. I was a go-getter (still am), and I didn't give up easily. This was especially true if it was something I wanted or if someone told me that they didn't think I could accomplish something. So imagine my surprise when in an employment review, my boss actually stated as an area of improvement that I needed to be more persistent. This came right after I worked so hard to put together a huge event where we partnered with Disney for a 10-year anniversary extravaganza. It was the biggest success that mall had seen and brought in tens of thousands of people. What? More persistent? Me? Anyone who knows me would probably laugh, as they know how driven I am. I told my boss I disagreed and proceeded to tell her all that I had to push through to make this event happen.

Now I see this boss was probably one of my greatest teachers and was re-emphasizing the very first lesson Sergei taught me: Be patiently persistent. Persistence is necessary, as is patience. It can play a big role in the outcome. Being narrowly driven or having a single-minded focus to push-push-push does not equate to efficiency or productivity.

Things were tough for me with Sergei in the beginning. Being a pet parent was an area where I had no experience. No matter how driven or persistent I was, I couldn't force him to be something he was not ready for. He was a puppy!

I couldn't make him learn any faster or grow out of certain unpleasant stages. People with children probably understand this better; you just have to get through it.

Patience, on the other hand, wasn't my strong suit. I was used to taking control and changing the means to the end, if that was necessary. In this case, and like what my boss was trying to say in my job review, the path to being steadfast and persevering is sometimes achieved through a bit of patience for the best outcome.

Now I know that through waiting and stillness, sometimes the most wonderful memories can be made. Better ideas or paths will present themselves that otherwise would have been missed. Training a puppy is not an overnight accomplishment. Pushing through or forcing to "make things happen" is not always the smartest way. I learned that my driven personality can relax a little and in doing so, I can enjoy life a little more. Things are going to happen whether I have control over them or not! Playful puppies are wonderful teachers.

Sergei's Lesson In Reflection

### Be patiently persistent.
Life is going to unfold in its own way and time. When we let go of trying to force outcomes, and instead relax and allow, everything is more peaceful.

*When Sergei was about six or seven months old*, I had to go out of state for a business trip. It would be the first time I was gone long enough to have to put him in a boarding kennel. At that time, I didn't have anyone who lived close by to stay with him. My work was paying for boarding as a trip expense, so I really didn't think twice about taking him to stay there.

I dropped Sergei off with a couple of toys and food and let them take him back to the crating area. I didn't talk to him or tell him when I would be back to pick him up. Sergei didn't have separation anxiety at home, so he just walked back with the woman in a happy prance.

When I picked Sergei up three days later, I was so surprised to see such a sad puppy turn the corner. His tail was down. He barely walked let alone prance. Then when his eyes met mine, wow! Instant happiness, tail wags, and yes... piddles on the floor. He jumped up and gave me so many kisses! At home, he instantly fell asleep on the floor in the sun—content and relieved. In fact, Sergei slept pretty much for the next 24 hours straight except to eat and go to the bathroom. At first, I thought he was sick.

Before I left for my trip, he wanted to play constantly. If I sat down, he was pushing at my elbow to get up and play. I then realized he hadn't slept much at all those three days! Sergei thought I had left him, and I felt horrible for having put him through that.

A few years later, an animal communicator told me how important it is to talk to our pets. "Let them know how long you will be gone. Tell them you love them and when you will return. Check in with them mentally while you are away to see how they are doing, and reaffirm how many 'moons' need to go by until you return." This made sense to me, so I tried it. It helped. I had to put Sergei in boarding kennels again when I traveled, and it was never as bad as that first time. However, I eventually came to the decision I wouldn't leave him in a kennel again, and he would have a pet sitter. Even though Sergei came to know that I would return, I wanted him to know his place was in our home, always.

As people, we know the importance of home. My parents divorced when I was six years old. I was too young to really understand what this meant, especially since my father continued to live with us for a while through the proceedings. After the divorce was final, my siblings and I saw my dad on weekends, which was probably more time than I had spent with him when he lived at home. My dad spent money on us to take us to the movies, to video arcades, to dinner… but he never truly talked to us or was emotionally available. He didn't talk about the divorce or about how that may affect us. I needed to know that he still loved me, would be there for me, and that he would never leave *me*.

Looking back, I can compare some of my feelings of abandonment from this childhood experience to how Sergei felt being left at the kennel that first time. The issue wasn't that my parents divorced. In fact, I think that was the healthiest thing for them both, and ultimately me and my siblings, but nobody talked about it. That was the problem. Every child wants to know they are loved and safe. You can never say that too much. Better yet, they *need* to know they are loved and safe. I needed to know that. Sergei needed to know that. We all need to know that. Talk to your loved ones, furry and not. Communicate. It matters.

Sergei's Lesson In Reflection

## Openly communicate.
It's the key to building trusting relationships. Never assume that loved ones know what you are thinking or feeling.

—⁂◯

*Anyone who knows Siberian Huskies knows they are runners.* They are working dogs and love physical as well as mental exercise. They also are known to have very little "homing" instinct. If they escape or are lost, it's not likely for a husky to find his way home after hours of exploration, sniffing, and seeing the sites. To be entirely safe from them bolting, the golden rule for this breed is to never let them off leash.

I was lucky. Sergei got out at least six times, both in my care and while in other's: A door left slightly open; an escape-artist from his collar on a walk; sneaking out of a picket-fenced yard between two posts that were rotted and not secure (yes, he found that the very first time in the yard!); and breaking through a screen door while I was in the shower.

When he got out, I was so scared that it must have been reflected in my voice, and he immediately would come when I called. However, when in the care of others he gave them a run for their money! Once he had someone chase him around a lake and another through a frog marsh pond. My mom had the greatest scare because she didn't even know he was gone.

Mom had not completely closed the front door. So when the screen door shut behind her, the air vacuum pushed the main door slightly open. This wouldn't have been a problem had the UPS delivery man not come by that day. When he opened the screen to place a package in the door, it left a direct route open from the house to the outside. Of course, Sergei found that opening and snuck out without my mom's knowledge. When she later came to check on him, she found Sergei gone!

Mom drove around the roads of the lakes we lived on, yelling his name, for over an hour. No luck. She later told me that she was so afraid for me to come home from work that day. She would have been heart-broken to have to tell me that she lost Sergei. Mom thought she had let me down—Sergei was on her watch, and her responsibility.

Angels must have been guiding Sergei that day because when my mom drove back, disheartened from her unsuccessful attempts to find him, Sergei was sitting pretty—right on the front porch, waiting! This is not typical for husky behavior, so I now know there was a lesson for me in his return.

I've had several places to call home. Usually I rented houses (as Sergei wasn't allowed in most apartment buildings), but my heart never truly was there to actually make it a home. I had moved seven times in twelve years, so maybe I never allowed myself to create such a home because I always knew it was temporary. Maybe it was because I always felt like I was searching in life, and I didn't want to put down roots that would make it hard to move on. Then I purchased a small condo. I painted the walls, some purple, some green, and I made it my own. It was then I finally recognized that a home has energy, and I honored that by silently "thanking" it when I came through the door everyday and felt happy to be there, safe, and nurtured. I finally made a home, and I felt the difference as I allowed myself to be supported by this space and re-energized from years of continual restlessness.

There is a quote that comes to mind as I write this, "No matter where you go, there you are." Running from one job, one place, one person to the next only delayed my inner unrest and instilled a sense of always being lost. I didn't realize I was running (always a gypsy so-to-speak), until I put down some roots. You don't have to go out and buy a home to have roots. In fact, even after purchasing my condo, I moved three years later, this time out of state, and rented again for the next seven years. But it wasn't until I gave myself permission to stay in one place without looking ahead to the next, to decorate the walls and make a home "in the now", did I allow myself the opportunity to truly rest, reflect, and have a foundation to start from in order to gain a perspective of what my next step should be for my best personal growth.

Sometimes we are like a dog: Simply being playful, wanting to explore, but searching for something outside ourselves for an answer, for a "home." We don't have to run away to find it. We all have a homing instinct. When we look within, we find our answers. It took me years to realize that. Our pets know and love the feeling of being home. So do humans.

*Sergei's Lesson In Reflection*

### Practice homing instincts.

Home may not be with relatives. It can be your own sacred space where you unwind, feel safe, and re-energize. It's exciting to go off and explore, but where is your foundation? Know the importance of home and come back to it often.

—⁂—

*There are health benefits to having a pet.* Studies prove it, but pet owners just know it. Pets can help reduce stress, anxiety, and even blood pressure. Many pets even become certified therapy dogs. Sergei was not designated officially as such, but he was definitely a therapy dog in his own way. He and I signed up for convalescent home visits, and I formed a local group for weekend visits to an assisted living group in Ann Arbor, Michigan.

At first I thought he was not right for that role. He didn't sit still at all during the visits! Sergei didn't calmly remain in a sit-stay while people pet his head. Instead, he happily wagged his tail and walked around the rooms sniffing everything. The people there would get a moment or two to interact with him, but then he'd move on to the next person or item that caught his interest (a big focus for him was the caged parakeet in the lobby). Needless to say, I was quite embarrassed because my dog wasn't "behaving." But I soon realized that the men and women who came in with lackluster energy and somber faces were smiling, talking, and even laughing. Sergei brought them to life! The elderly enjoyed his energy, and it uplifted their spirits. These folks didn't need more calm in their life; they need stimulation, and Sergei was the perfect dog for this role. He provided healing to them just as laughter is healing for the soul.

When I moved from my condo, Sergei and I didn't continue to do these visits elsewhere, as most retirement or assisted living homes required the official therapy dog certification. I knew that wasn't meant for Sergei. His spirit wasn't meant to be confined to expected behaviors. Before moving, he did have one last visiting therapy mission. It was to see my Uncle Chuck during his last few days on this earth. My uncle was suffering from cancer, and he had been moved to something similar to a hospice facility that allowed pets. My mom and I went to visit him.

I had not seen Uncle Chuck in about nine years, as he was estranged from my mom after my grandfather's passing. During this visit, all the past seemed to melt away, and I was happy that he and my mom were able to show love for each other again. He recognized me and smiled. He physically couldn't speak as the cancer had affected his lungs and throat. Sergei, normally the active boy as I described above, must have realized the seriousness of Uncle Chuck's health as he simply walked right up to the bed, put his front paws up, and tried to get as close as possible to my uncle. I lifted Sergei onto the bed. Yes, this 75-pound dog wanted to lay beside my uncle and give him kisses.

I had recently been certified as a Reiki Master and helped my uncle prepare for crossing that day. With everyone in that room just being true to themselves and not listening to the ego's sense of pride, revenge, or bitterness, tremendous healing occurred for both my mom and my uncle. Sergei's and my healing efforts, and my uncle's unspoken reconciliation with my mom were powerful. My uncle's soul was finally ready to cross, which he did soon thereafter—peacefully.

**Stay true to you.** Don't force yourself into a role just because it's expected of you. Your spirit will flourish by being genuine, and others will also benefit, sometimes in the most unexpected ways.

*It had been over two years since I had seen my ex-boyfriend.*
We had dated on and off for a couple of years first and
then exclusively for three more. I had thought at the time
we were soul mates, and I truly anticipated Fred and I
would get married. Oh, and he loved Sergei! Fred is the
man from the first story of the Fourth of July fateful newspaper listing. He drove up to my place to see Sergei the
day after I got him. When they met, Sergei was under-
neath a bench swing that I was sitting on in the back yard.
(Remember, this was within the first week where Sergei
seemed to sleep all the time.) Fred and the serene Sergei
were instant pals. Since Fred and I had just re-connected,
we felt like Sergei was our child.

Fred and I had a great relationship. We laughed, we
talked, and we were in sync on so many levels. But after
three years, Fred was still uncertain about taking the next
step. I never pushed marriage. In fact, he brought it up
more than I did. One day he would talk about our future,
but the next day back-pedal saying he didn't know if he
could ever commit to anyone. I was not one to give ultima-
tums, so I enjoyed our time together and even accepted his
uncertainty thinking it would one day change.

Instead of a change in his attitude there was a shift in mine. I mean, if he was uncertain after three years in a wonderful, healthy relationship, I was fooling myself thinking it would be different after marriage, assuming he ever decided to go down that road with me. One day I just knew I had enough, that things would not change, and I broke up with him. Just like that, we were done. Because of our quick breakup, Fred never got to say goodbye to his friend, Sergei.

For weeks and even months afterwards, it wasn't easy to stay apart. I often missed Fred's company and all of the good parts of our relationship. I had to remind myself that although I missed these things, what I really missed was the vision of what I *wanted* with him versus what we had. I had to trust that there had to be someone out there better for me and for him.

A lot happened in the years that passed after our breakup. The main one is that Fred got married! I was truly happy for him that he found someone, and also in knowing that obviously we were not meant to be together. We had had a difficult breakup, emotionally. Neither of us really had healthy closure, so I invited him to lunch and to see Sergei again to get closure with him too. Sergei definitely remembered Fred and gave him a very excited welcome. This momentary reunion with him ended quickly, as Fred had come just to say his final goodbye. As Fred turned to leave, Sergei didn't follow him but stayed sitting. He let out a unique whimper as he watched Fred leave; it was a sound I had never heard from Sergei before. If he could speak, I imagine he would have been saying, "I know we will never see each other again, and I will truly miss you, my dear friend." It was a sound I would never forget. I felt Sergei was validating my actions two years earlier. He didn't run after Fred. He just knew it wasn't meant to be.

That was the first time that I had been the one to end a relationship. Not to get Freudian here, but issues with my dad's aloofness and inability to commit, even to me as his daughter, led me to choose relationships throughout my life that mirrored the inability to receive. It was a necessary step for me to break this relationship pattern. In the past, I would be unhappy in a relationship, but stick it out hoping for change. I would feel like a doormat, or eventually be the one to be dumped. I had broken off a relationship only one other time–my first love, actually–but only after I found a love note he wrote to another woman. Why did I always wait? I knew I wasn't happy, yet I just yearned for acceptance.

Did I have any revelations of this self-discovery the day I broke up with Fred? No. It took me five more years on my journey to realize this. That's when I met Phillip, my now husband, and it was well worth the wait.

Sergei's whimper of goodbye to Fred reminds me that often the right choice for self-growth can be the most difficult one. Choosing our best path is not always easy. If it were, it wouldn't be a life lesson, and then the cycle would continue. I had to recognize the subtleties of my situation and act out of self-love. A dog's love can be the jumpstart to finding that self-love giving us courage to let go and say goodbye peacefully.

*Sergei's Lesson In Reflection*

**Saying goodbye is okay.** Whether people leave your life by your choice or not, be strong and know that for every ending a wonderful new beginning is waiting.

*Pet lovers know that animals can be great company.* Sometimes, they are the only companions we have in life. This was my case when Sergei and I moved from Michigan to Florida. I was moving, but I had no idea where to! I had narrowed it down by internet research to the gulf-side of Florida between Venice and Bradenton. In fact, my movers didn't have a physical address of where to deliver my belongings. They were instructed to call me when they arrived in Florida, as they may be delivering everything to a storage unit. What an adventure for me! I was in my early 30s and felt like I was just finding myself.

My first day of driving I heard the song *Here I Go Again* by Whitesnake on the radio (oldies station!). I started singing and dancing in my car to the lyrics. I could relate. I too didn't know where I was going but I sure knew where I'd been. I felt empowered. I was again on my own, and it did "feel like the only road I had ever known."

Just like they sang, I had made up mind and wasn't going to waste more time. Yup, I was off to start my own marketing and design business wherever I decided to settle. My dog by my side was all I needed. He was my protector and best-buddy in my travels. Life was good!

I don't remember where we stayed for the first night, but I wanted to take it easy and stop when it was still light. Once at the hotel, I rollerbladed with Sergei for his exercise and mine, and was surprised to find myself all done and settled in our room by 8 p.m. As I lay still for all of maybe five minutes, I became bored. With that boredom, my mind wandered to things that made me feel lonely. Suddenly the lyrics of the song I sang to earlier with zest and life now made me cry. Here I was on my own "again," with again being the operative word. It truly was just me and Sergei in the world at that moment. Wow, I had gone from a personal high to a personal low in a matter of maybe six hours! Sergei was there to nuzzle me while I cried.

The next day I took it easy driving and decided to stop in Georgia. Having to find a pet-friendly hotel that was economical, I ended up in a poorer side of the city. At a traffic light about a block away from the hotel, Sergei sat up and looked out the window. There was a homeless man and his dog keeping cool in the shade below an overpass. I had a box of dog bones in my front seat, so I rolled down my window and asked if I could give one to his dog. "Sure," the man said. Then he turned to his companion and said, "At least you have dinner tonight, buddy." He thanked me, turned away, and headed back to his blanket. Wow. He didn't ask me for money. He didn't ask me for anything. He was happy his dog had food, however small it was.

His dog was his only companion, too. It sure put my troubles into perspective as I drove off. I was sad and scared about my situation, but how must this man feel? Thinking of someone else helped me to overcome my self-pity and feel compassion for another. It was as if Sergei knew I needed to interact with this man to help in my own healing. If it weren't for my dog sitting up to take notice, I probably would have driven right on by. Dogs help us to be aware and in the moment.

I drove to the nearest grocery store and bought a roasted chicken, a loaf of French bread, and a gallon of water to bring back to the man. For his dog, I had some more of Sergei's treats and food. The man remembered me and came up to the car. He took the items gratefully but not in an overly excited way like I had expected. He was kind and reverent. Here was a man living for the moment. He trusted in life, grateful for what he would receive, but not worried about anything other than the present. I drove by a little while later and saw that he was sharing his meal with another homeless man. That too made me feel good.

I don't know about you, but I have a tendency to focus on the me-factor. What am "I" going to do? How can "I" get what "I" want? Where am "I" going in life to make "me" happy? Sergei wanted me to see this gentleman and his dog that day for a reason. I had a lesson to learn. Here was a man and his dog, with far less than I had, and I thought I was homeless at that point in time because of having no address or place to call home. But that was temporary. This man was living on the streets. Through Sergei's eyes, I gained perspective. Everything is relative in life. My problems were certainly real, but by appreciating someone else's problems, I took the focus off of me and on to another person in need. It was just one meal and one day. Perhaps seemingly insignificant to most, but not to this man nor to me. This brief interaction taught me a lifetime lesson in how to make my life more complete through compassion. It also solidified the importance of our canine friends. They are there for us when nobody else is, on whatever road we're on, waiting, ready to serve. Dogs sound like earth angels, don't they? We know they are.

*Sergei's Lesson In Reflection*

**Keep perspective.** Our ups and downs in life are important, but remember they're also relative. Taking the focus off of ourselves and being compassionate to others can lift self-burden, bring a higher perspective of understanding, and with that, peace.

*My first day with Sergei! In Port Huron, Michigan.*

*Sergei under the swing with Fred. That first week, all he did was sleep.*

*Sergei at 4-years-old, behind my condo in Ann Arbor, Michigan.*

*Sergei with my friend, Colleen. This was during my move to Florida,*
*before I had an address or a place to call home.*

*A drawing from a retirement home resident gifted to me during one of Sergei's therapy dog visits. Mr. Hawker drew this only from memory of Sergei!*

*Sergei with my mom, Laura. She came to visit us in Sarasota,
Florida before she was diagnosed again with lung cancer.*

*Sergei giving me my "daily dose of joy"
after we had moved back to Michigan.*

*Sergei enjoying his 9ᵗʰ birthday with our family during an Easter celebration, the last one spent with my mom.*

*My Happily Ever After! Sergei with me and my husband, Phillip. Even though Sergei could not be my "best man" at my wedding, we made sure he was in all of our engagement photos.*

*Me & Sergei, my greatest teacher*

*Sergei was a happy dog and very discerning.* You've probably heard one of the common lessons we can learn from dogs is to "bark less—wag more." Sergei certainly wasn't a barker, but he was also very discerning with his big tail wags; he saved them up for certain people. Pizza delivery drivers could come to the door, and Sergei would come explore, but not bark. Even on walks he didn't bark at other dogs. I always felt like doing so would be "beneath" him of sorts, like he was an old soul who had already experienced the lessons of physical protection. He had "been-there-done-that!" Rather, Sergei had an inner sense of danger. Not just for danger, but an intuition for people and their true intentions.

There were only two times that I experienced Sergei in full-on protection mode, where he not only barked, but howled like only Siberian Huskies do. Both times were late at night. The first event was a knock on my bedroom window at 2 a.m. I didn't know anybody who would do that at that hour. My gut told me not to open the window, as Sergei went into that howl-bark mode. I called the police and they said, "Miss, it sounds like you have the best protection with you there in the house!" By the time the police got there, they found nothing. Was it somebody who knocked on the wrong house? A prank? Maybe I avoided something a little more sinister. Who knows? All I know is that Sergei was there as my protector.

The second time was uncannily similar, except this was a year or two later after I had moved to Sarasota, Florida (where I settled after my move from Michigan). Same time of night, but this time it was at the front door. I had only been renting this house for a couple of months and didn't know anyone yet. The Sergei alarm went off again. This time I didn't call the police, remembering how Sergei had scared off the intruder years before. After the knocks stopped, Sergei soon quieted down. I was later told by my landlord, who had just finished completely renovating this small cottage before I moved in, that the place had been empty for years and used to be a drug house. Nice! Now you tell me.

Sergei and I left that house after a year and moved into a beautiful upper-level rental in the Sarasota Arts District. The bottom was an art studio that was not lived in and only open during the day. I loved the place but worried that Sergei would have trouble with the stairs since he had become very lethargic while living at the "drug house," not even jumping up on my bed anymore. Nope! He literally ran up the stairs in our new place, just like a puppy! His demeanor totally changed. The energy of this home was so different, so light, and so positive. My buoyant playful dog had returned. I truly feel that the heavy, lower energies of that rental cottage had affected him physically. I hadn't given it much thought until I experienced how different and wonderful the new place felt, to both of us. The cottage had been renovated; everything was brand new. It was decorated by an artist, so it looked nice. The heaviness of that house had more to do with something other than the interior or the surroundings. It was the energy of the place. We were both glad to be free of it and, needless to say, now that we were on the second floor—no more knocks on windows or doors in the middle of the night.

I had no idea my surroundings were affecting me emotionally, and Sergei physically, until I experienced something better. I hadn't used my discernment when renting that house. It looked so artsy and appealing with its art deco décor and newly renovated interior. I had only looked at the physical and thought it would be good to live there. Of course, it's easy to see things more clearly looking in hindsight.

As I reflect now with the wisdom of Sergei's eyes, I feel strongly that the lesson is more than just using discernment. Sergei exercised discernment in knowing who merited a bark from him versus a full-on howl. We humans know sentiments that speak to this, like "Don't bite when a growl will do." Sometimes we don't even need to growl. So often we jump right to action from judgment. Be it a person, a place, or a situation, we judge when instead we can practice discernment. Judgment is ego-based. Discernment is spiritually-based, and I do not mean religion. Discernment is what helps us see through pretenses to the truth. It guides us out of situations that are no longer beneficial into new ones that will better serve us and our happiness.

Picture a dog sniffing around, checking things out. They're able to discern through that sense. We too can refrain from snap judgments and take a moment to "sniff around," sensing to see if this is the right person or opportunity for us. It means we have to pay attention. We have to trust. You won't know how much better life can be until you let go of judgment and practice discernment!

**Use discernment over judgment.** It will help you to use your energy wisely and steer you toward healthier situations.

*When I lived in Florida, I would take Sergei for walks around our neighborhood.* It was the first time I really experienced mockingbirds. I know we had them in Michigan, but they weren't as prevalent, or at least I never seemed to notice them. In Sarasota, however, they would dive-bomb Sergei—just barely missing his head! After reading up on them, I learned this was a protection mechanism as mockingbirds are very territorial of their nests. We never walked near a nest that I saw, but obviously we were in what they considered close range.

The dive-bombing frightened me, and I would wave my arms to try to get them away from Sergei. They didn't swoop in on me—just Sergei—and I wanted to protect him. What always amazed me was that Sergei never missed a step. He acted like the birds weren't even there and just kept walking. Did he notice? He had to, I thought. He's a dog! He notices everything. Sergei simply handled them better than me. Their swooping and dive-bombing never broke his stride.

Have you ever had someone in your life tell you an idea would never work? Or belittle you for wanting to follow your dreams? They say things like, "That won't pay the bills!" or "Be reasonable, that's a long-shot; the likelihood of success is near impossible!" These people are like those mockingbirds, dive-bombing you. They feel threatened because they don't understand your path. They are fearful, whether they admit it (or realize it) or not. Their words and actions often feel like an attack.

I've had people in my life who thought they were protecting me. In truth, they were trying to protect themselves. They were threatened that I had the courage to follow my heart and be happy when they lacked that same courage. They didn't want to be left alone in their misery! Those who tried to discourage me were reacting in order to protect themselves and the status quo—just like the mockingbirds. Yes, even our loved ones do this to us. They probably do it even more often than anyone else because we are the closest to them and are a very real and close reminder that they may not be living out their own calling to happiness.

Similarly, when others attacked me for my decisions, it was human nature for me to want to defend myself (like I did on behalf of Sergei by waving and shooing the birds away). That can easily turn into a never-ending battle of who's right and who's wrong. Instead, I choose to take a higher perspective and simply let them have their beliefs. It's sometimes difficult to not be on the counter-attack and defend my reasons, but in the grand scheme of things all that would do is let their negative energy into my space and pull me down. When the mockingbirds attacked Sergei, he did not snap at them. He did not even look at them! He kept on walking and enjoying the scenery and his pursuits.

If you're like me and find yourself in a situation where you feel the need to explain yourself, I've learned it helps to keep it simple. For example, you can say something like, "I'm sorry you feel that way as I would really like your support, but this is what will make me happy. It's the path I need to take, or at least try, for me."

Others may call you selfish for your behavior. That is their last-ditch effort to keep you with them in their misery, hoping guilt will change your path. A final dive-bomb before retreat. If what you are choosing to do is a result of inspiration, reflection, and speaks from the heart, it is never selfish! Trust that inner guidance. It doesn't always turn out that the first journey on the road to self-discovery is "it." I personally took several paths that I thought were my final destination. Not so. Each one, however, provided a valuable learning lesson. Each and every path in hindsight was a blessing. (Yes, every one! Even when trying or challenging.) They led me to make a turn, to course-correct, and ultimately to my goal. I just had to keep taking one step at a time, as we rarely see our final destination until we arrive. Like Sergei, don't let the dive-bombers stop us in our tracks. Sergei kept walking, and stayed happy all along the way.

**Focus on your path.** Don't let others deter you from your goals. Often, they have a misperception or are simply fearful themselves.

*Here I was, moving again.* Not completely sure about moving from Sarasota back to Michigan, I decided to spend the month of December back with my mom, who of course was excited and welcomed me and Sergei with open arms.

I was looking forward to it, but my spirit dampened quickly as one thing after another happened. The first day of the long road trip started out sunny, but the sun set early this time of year, and I found myself in a torrential downpour right in time for my drive through downtown Atlanta. Traffic halted in my lane to almost a standstill, but cars in other lanes were flying by above the speed limit. My knuckles were white as I gripped the wheel, not only worried about my safety but mostly for Sergei who was in the back seat. There were accidents all around us. I found myself praying for protection and for angels to guide us to safety. This went on for maybe an hour, and my energy was so depleted from worry and strain that by the time I got to the hotel for the night, I was spent. I know Sergei sensed my stressful emotions, but he happily jumped up on the bed as soon as we got there. He was content and happy for a dry, soft bed, and we cuddled and fell asleep until morning. The events of the day before must have worn my body down a bit too much because the next day's drive was accompanied by a cold. Not too bad at first, but it had progressed into a full-blown flu by day three. It really wasn't the welcome home I was hoping for.

No rest for the weary as I tried to continue working while at my mom's. One client wanted a logo created and some graphic design projects done as a rush job. I knew I should have said no and rested, but I was thinking of the money and didn't want to lose the client. In the end, she didn't even pay me for the work. I took this as the last sign (one of many over the last several months) that this career was not the right path for me anymore. I had absolutely no clue what I would do next, but I decided I wasn't going back to live in Sarasota. Although not easy, I had an inner sense that things would work out.

During this stay, my mom told me that her doctor had found a spot on her lung that they wanted to "watch." This was after she had lung surgery for cancer almost five years prior. She wouldn't listen to my suggestion to get a second opinion. I feel I should have been more adamant, and maybe she would have been alive to see me get married just two years later.

I stayed with her longer than the month of December, and in February she was officially diagnosed again, this time with squamous cell lung cancer. I became her caregiver, living with her fulltime, declaring bankruptcy in the process. Over the course of these months, it seemed my life was taken from the book title, *A Series of Unfortunate Events.* Where is Sergei in this story? Right beside me the whole time. He gave me a little bit of joy every day in a time of my life that I otherwise would not have looked for it.

Sergei and I would go on long walks in the snow on trails through the woods, and he would leap into large snow drifts like a reindeer. I called him Prancer, and my body could not help but laugh and smile at him. He would roll on his back and make doggy snow angels. His bright blue eyes would smile at me when he was having so much fun. Yes, I said his eyes would smile because they would light up differently than usual, saying "Just for today, mom, do not worry." It's one of the five precepts from my Reiki training that is so important. Just for today, do not worry. Sergei made my heart light, even if it was for only 45 minutes a day.

There have been other times in my life that I'd consider myself going through a dark night of the soul – a scary time of despair where all seemed lost. This happened quite a bit throughout the decade of my twenties between failed jobs and failed relationships. One time my depression was so intense that I considered, for a fleeting moment, if taking my own life would be a solution.

Thankfully, I kept faith that I had purpose. My life is so blessed now, and I would never have dreamed of the path that was paved for me would lead to so much gratitude and joy. Sometimes the hill we have to climb lasts a week. Sometimes a decade. But either way, they are both overcome just one day at a time. Daily joy keeps us focused on the present. I'm so grateful to have had Sergei to be my support dog through that transitional time with my mom, and to remind me, "Just for today, do not worry."

**Find joy daily.** Or let it find you! A small beacon of light can help you through some of the more difficult times life can bring.

*My mom had smoked since she was a teenager.* The habit never took up with me or my three siblings. We constantly asked her to stop, but her answer was always, "When I'm ready." She finally quit smoking, but as you know from the last story, she developed lung cancer. The ironic part is that it was just six months after her last cigarette, at age 60, that she was diagnosed for the first time. One-quarter of her lung was surgically removed, but no chemotherapy was performed; they thought it all was removed.

This first time with cancer, Mom seemed to recover well. Our family went on a Christmas cruise with all but one of my brothers and his family. The eight of us had a wonderful time. My mom always loved Disney, and she posed with the characters and became a kid again on this 7-day adventure. That was the last vacation we all went on together as the cancer recurred just shy of the five-year clear mark.

Mom had told me about the doctor finding a spot on her lung, but the final diagnosis of the metastasized cancer was announced by Mom at my sister's house a couple of months later. Sergei happened to be there with me. I held my tears until I was in the car with him driving home. Once out of sight from the others, the tears and sobs flowed freely. This was a different feeling from the first diagnosis years before. I knew in my soul she would not survive this time.

Sergei was in the back seat, and he felt the difference in my sobs and started to climb through the two front seats to get into my lap. Even as a puppy, Sergei was never a lap dog. He would give kisses and know when I was upset, but never to the extent of this day. I was driving, so of course this was dangerous as he offered to console me.

I tried to tell him I was "okay," and gently use my arm to get him into the back seat once again. He didn't buy it. He kept coming and would get his front paws into my lap. It wasn't until I internally calmed myself down a bit, took a deep breath, and thanked him that he returned to the back seat.

Why is it human nature to push people away at our most trying times? I know when I feel vulnerable, I fear letting others see my weakness. I didn't show my feelings to my mom that day. I never really showed them to her thinking I had to be strong for her sake. But by doing that, I didn't allow my mom to show her vulnerability either. She must have been so scared! By my putting up an "optimistic" wall, she didn't feel she could let her real feelings show either. Even in Mom's last moments, I was telling her facts such as, "The hospice house has a walk-in bath tub. You can finally take a bath again!" I couldn't share my emotions or bring myself to tell her how much I would miss her, or cry at her bedside. In hindsight, I wish I had. Sergei was showing me that day in the car that it's okay to release and share painful emotions because those who care about you will respond to console. It's a healing for both sides. Even if you don't know how to accept that gift at that moment in time, a simple thank you will do.

## Show vulnerability.

Letting others help you, especially when you are most vulnerable, is healing for you as well as the giver. If you are truly unable to accept their gift at that moment, a simple thank you will go a long way.

—◦♫◦—

*When Sergei met my husband for the first time,* I knew Phillip was a special person. Sergei was giving me his approval. We were all in my mom's driveway when their first meeting happened. Sergei went right up, tail wagging full force, and stood up placing his front paws on Phillip—both paws right on his heart. Now granted, this may seem like normal behavior for some dogs, but not for Sergei. He was a very friendly dog, yes, but he was more what I would call aloof. He would simply acknowledge people with a quick glance or a tail wag or two, and then walk away turning his interest to nature or whatever else he could examine around him. Unless, that is, he had a distinct first impression about someone. Then his actions could be seen either as one of approval or a warning.

For Phillip's greeting, Sergei had never done this to any person in my life. It was a positive sign and one of importance because of how out of character it was. Earlier symbols of Sergei's first impressions of others had been more of disapproval. For example, we went to a veterinarian in Michigan I really liked, but on one particular visit we didn't get his regular vet. Instead, a woman walked into the room. I'd never met her before, and I'm sure she was a great vet, but my heart sank as I learned we weren't seeing the main doctor who both Sergei and I really liked. No sooner had this new vet started talking to us when Sergei walked over to her, lifted his leg, and relieved himself. I was so embarrassed! Again, he had never done that before. I'm sure she is a wonderful veterinarian; she just wasn't the right one for us at the time. She continued with her exam, but her diagnosis was inconclusive. When we went back the following week to see the veterinarian we both liked, he was able to quickly pinpoint Sergei's issue, which ended up being borderline diabetes.

How often have you had first impressions that you wish you would have paid attention to at that time? Maybe you saw a person that you felt a soul connection with, but didn't go up to say hello and still think about that person years later? Or you get a feeling of distrust for a seemingly well-natured person who turned out to do you wrong?

It's human nature to discount our gut feelings because we think we're not being rational. I still try and things. It seems more mature somehow to make a neat pro/con list and take the logical path. So often we don't include our feelings or intuition in the mix, when that is by far the most important factor to consider. I have learned to trust my intuition, accepting it's the vehicle our higher self and the universe use to communicate. Both have our highest good in mind, which is why we can always trust those feelings. Still, so many of us discount our first impressions because we rationalize that we must be wrong because there's nothing to confirm them. I'm not saying to jump without a net, or to make a scene when you meet someone you don't trust. Definitely don't pee on their leg! But you can recognize if it's your intuition telling you something by the feeling it gives either to your heart or to your gut.

*Sergei's Lesson In Reflection*

**Trust first impressions.**
Pay attention to your gut instincts, even subtle ones. Trust your intuition; it's always guiding you to your highest good.

*I had always said I wanted Sergei to be my "man of honor" at my wedding.* After all, whoever was going to marry me was going to marry my dog! Like many women, I liked to envision that day with hope one day my prince would come. He did.

Although I didn't expect anyone to come riding in on a white horse to sweep me off of my feet, I also didn't expect to be that cliché that makes most of us roll our eyes: "You'll find love when you least expect it." To top that off, when I first met Phillip I was probably at my lowest point emotionally and physically. So when Phillip's first word to me was a simple "yup" as he turned away, I let it slide. I was trying to be cordial and introduce myself as the one playing the role of Babette to his casted role of Lumiere in a community theater play of *Beauty and the Beast*. I didn't have my normal chutzpa for a comeback to his aloofness. I just turned and rolled my eyes. I'll refrain from listing my exact first thoughts of this man who became my husband two years later, but it was something to the likes of, "What a jerk!" I was not looking for love at that time. In fact, we both needed a little help from the universe over the next several months to align it for us.

All of this happened after moving back to care for my mom. I had left Sarasota, folded my business, declared bankruptcy, and had an onset of vertigo that was on its second month straight by that time (part of my series of unfortunate events). On the positive side, I had just started a marketing director position at the University of Michigan. On my drive back to my mom's house each night, I passed a sandwich board advertising auditions for the musical.

I had never been in a musical. In fact, I was embarrassed to sing! I had taken and taught dance for more than 15 years, but I never would have given any thought to audition. Yet my head turned to look at that sign every day on the way home—like a magnet. I would be driving deep in thought, watching the road, and my eyes would turn to look at that board... every, single, time. As if that wasn't a sign, one night my mom suggested that I look into doing something at the theater to get involved (it was literally right across the street from her subdivision). She knew I was not feeling well and thought it would get me out of the house and away from my troubles at hand. The odd thing is, neither of us were theater people. When I took her to see *Phantom of the Opera* in Toronto years before, she almost didn't go saying, "I don't like opera!" and the same for Cirque de Soleil, "I don't like the circus!" So you see, this was uncharacteristic of something she would suggest.

I took note of these coincidences and went to offer my choreography services to the director. Somehow, I ended up auditioning, pushed into it actually, as an ultimatum for my being able to choreograph. The rest you know; I was cast as Babette, and Phillip was cast for Lumiere. Remember the story when Sergei met Phillip? That was during a cast party just a few months later. The rest, as they say, is the *Happily Ever After* I had always dreamed about but was searching for in all the wrong places with the wrong men. The best part is that I still can't believe it all happened when I wasn't even looking! 2017 is our ten-year anniversary, and all I can say is it absolutely was worth the wait and all of my past heartaches.

Sergei's part in this story is more than just one incident but more of a collaboration of events over the next few years. Phillip and I moved in together, and he and Sergei immediately bonded. We moved twice in one year ending up in the Winston-Salem area of North Carolina just one week before our wedding. We got married on a cruise ship with close family and friends, so my dream of Sergei being my man of honor could not come to be, but his health would not have let him anyway. In the next two weeks after we got home from our cruise, Sergei was diagnosed with diabetes and also needed ACL surgery. It was my new full-time job that we had moved for, so Phillip stayed at home to take care of Sergei. Their bond grew stronger as a result. Phillip took on the role of nurse to my "son" as I had done for Mom. He definitely became Sergei's dad. About a year later, Sergei lost his sight to cataracts, and we opted to get him surgery to enrich the last years of his life.

I'm not quite sure how to put into words this time period of Sergei's and my life. It was as if he knew Phillip was now becoming my rock, my life partner, and he was slowly backing away, letting go through life's natural journey. He and Phillip were close, which was so important to me. It may seem sad of course, but in reflection, it's beautiful poetic timing. There were no coincidences in my life's plan, and Sergei was still teaching me, and now Phillip, even further compassion for pets and for situations that would guide us after he was gone. Sergei may not have been able to be at my wedding, and my mom was only able to be there in spirit as she had passed away the year before, but both definitely were present in my heart for my happy ending.

Sergei's Lesson In Reflection

## Know that love evolves.
Love may change over time, but it always remains. Those you love are always a part of you.

*For my fortieth birthday, my husband and I took Sergei with us to Charleston, South Carolina.* Sergei was a traveling dog and did very well in the car. It was May, so he had to stay in the hotel a lot because of the heat. Mid to upper ninety degrees, much too hot for him to be walking about. We'd take him for short walks early in the morning down to The Battery and White Park Garden where there were lots of trees for shade. Sergei couldn't walk very far anymore. He had just turned twelve the month before, and the ACL surgery a couple years earlier wasn't exactly successful. He still loved to get outdoors and oh, how he loved the smell of the water! After all, he had grown up on Lake Huron and had lived at the lake with me and Mom. He was very at home around water.

As we were leaving to head back home from our short weekend-getaway, I had this unexplainable feeling. Before we got on the highway, we drove back to the water at The Battery that Sergei so loved. Sergei stuck his head out of the window, sniffing...sniffing and gave a bit of a quick whine. I knew that whine. It was the same one given to Fred the last time he saw him and said goodbye.

Sergei was saying goodbye to this place. He knew he wouldn't be back, and part of me realized this but didn't want to admit it. What I didn't know is that he would only be with us another ten short weeks. In hindsight, I wish we had stayed longer in Charleston, even just another hour or two to let Sergei out of the car to take it all in one last time. Instead, we followed our human timetable of getting on the road.

Life without regrets. I would love that. Wouldn't we all? I regret not following my instincts to stay longer in Charleston and letting Sergei "smell the roses" longer. Maybe a small regret, but it serves as an important lesson for me to seize the day for the life ahead of me, and to spend as much time as possible with the people I love.

I consider myself blessed that I have few regrets in life, but I still haven't fully forgiven myself for the ones I do have. It's time I do so. Dogs certainly don't live in the past. They live for the moment. Sergei's lesson to me here is to appreciate the moments we wish to cherish, and to let go of the past without guilt.

**Live without regrets.**
Before acting on auto-pilot for routines or self-imposed timetables, take a moment to listen to your heart and hear what is truly your most important task of the day. Then seize it!

⟿⨎⟲

*Sergei was with me over twelve years.* These stories I've shared are only a handful of the memories I have with him and the lessons he personally has taught me. I called him my "rock" because he was always grounding, steady, and would carry me through some of my most trying times. If I cried, he put his head on my lap. If I was scared, he would protect me. Always by my side, to me he projected an image like that of a magnificent, white stallion with a flowing mane; his energy was beautiful and significantly present—almost royal. Losing Sergei created a void in my life that can't be filled, but it has also taken me on a wonderful journey.

Sergei's last week on this earth I felt useless and helpless because I couldn't save him, as he had done for me his whole life. My husband had traveled out of town to visit family, a rare occurrence without me, and I had stayed home to watch over Sergei. He needed daily insulin shots and was too old to travel the 10-hour drive. By this time in his life, Sergei had partial facial paralysis from a stroke he must have suffered (unbeknownst to me except this physical sign). We had to give him daily eye drops as a result and daily ear drops to help keep the ear canal cleansed from a bacterium that was completely resistant to all antibiotics. The only cure would have been ear surgery; something I didn't want to put him through at his age. However, this week I had decided to get his ears cleaned under anesthesia. The vet confirmed ear drum damage and cleaned them out the best he could. On the way home Sergei was alert, and I bought him a fast-food hamburger (just the beef patty because of his diabetes). After that, however, it was the unfortunate start of the end.

He laid on the floor all of the next day. I had assumed it was still an after-effect of the anesthesia, but then he stopped eating and drinking, and started panting heavily and would not move. I couldn't lift him into the car, so the vet's office came to pick him up. They treated him with fluids all day and did many, many tests. Nothing showed. He was a little stronger, but after he returned home, he started having seizures, probably because his insulin was off from not eating properly. Needless to say, I called for my husband to come home. We put shower curtains and padding under Sergei to absorb the urine as he had seizures. We stayed up all night with him waiting for a final test to come back from the vet that had to be sent out (Rocky Mountain spotted fever). I talked to Sergei and told him to hold on for me. I asked him not to go until we knew if there was a treatment! Looking back, I wish I had not done that for that's exactly what he did. He held on. He even wouldn't have a seizure in front of me. I know that sounds like something out of his control, but somehow he would hold off for hours. Then only when I absolutely had to leave the room would I come back to him recovering from an episode.

After I got the results back from the vet as negative, and seeing the heartbreaking decline of my beloved Sergei, I finally told him he could let go. As soon as I said that he became pretty much unconscious. He wouldn't respond to my touch, to water, or even lick a bit of tequila that I had put on my finger (he had refined taste!). It was about 10 p.m., and I couldn't bear it any longer. With the help of our neighbor, we took Sergei to the emergency vet to be euthanized. He was already gone—it was just his body that remained, and it was in pain. We said our goodbyes to him. Just one breath after the injection, and his body was at peace.

Sergei and my mom both passed away after I verbally talked to them, out loud, letting them know it was okay to pass. I told them that I would miss them terribly, but they needed to go and be out of pain. Letting go can be our biggest challenge where death is concerned. Even harder still for those who don't have the opportunity to say goodbye from sudden or unexpected illnesses or accidents. For me, even though I believe the soul of both humans and animals alike live on, death has been the greatest challenge for me in letting go. Maybe it's the physical finality of it.

Letting go for me has been difficult in other areas as well, past jobs, boyfriends, and other experiences. In retrospect, I wouldn't change anything. My series of failed jobs or relationships just pushed me closer to my purpose and ultimate happiness. I had to learn when to move on and stop hitting my head against a brick wall. I would have never guessed in a million years that I would be running a non-profit organization that helps people save the lives of their family pets. Had it not been for these brick walls or the rock-bottom experiences in my life, I would not have been driven to seek the companionship of a dog in the first place. I would have never experienced the life lessons Sergei ended up teaching me, ultimately allowing me to finally find my path and realize my ultimate final lesson from him... that being of service to others and living a compassionate life is the secret ingredient for the alchemy of happiness.

Sergei's Lesson In Reflection

**Learn when to let go.**
Whether it's a relationship, unhealthy situation, or a loved one during their time of transition, letting go doesn't mean forgetting. It clears the way for a wonderful beginning.

# EPILOGUE

# Epilogue

Sergei died on August 13, 2009. His death immediately left a void in my life and my husband's. Unexpectedly, it also left a sense of guilt from having to euthanize him. This ache of guilt made me want to help others avoid this self-sabotaging anxiety. If I felt this way knowing all that we did to try to help Sergei, how much worse it must be for someone who has to say goodbye to their beloved family pet, not because of age or natural timing, but because they truly have no ability to pay for life-saving surgery.

My love for Sergei was precious and life changing. He touched me deeply and made a difference in my life. I know others feel the same about their pets. My personal experience and the pain of losing Sergei fueled my passion to start a charity to help people in their efforts to save their sick and injured pets. The very next day after his passing, The Sergei Foundation was founded with a mission of "Saving companion pets' lives by providing veterinary financial aid to families unable to afford emergency, life-saving care."

Hopefully, you are lucky enough to never have experienced the helplessness or hopeless feelings of not being able to care for a pet in need. For those who have, it's more than losing a pet and family member. Guilt, depression and even physical ailments caused from stress are often inflicted on the whole family. By providing a helping hand at a time when it is needed most, The Sergei Foundation is a beacon of hope to these families in times of greatest need. The gratitude from those who have been assisted is profound, and healing comes not only to the pet, but also to the entire family.

Like many things in life, the effort to create and grow this organization was not a seamless one. The year after its formation, I was laid off from my full-time job. I collected unemployment while worrying that our house would be foreclosed. I attempted to go back to work three separate times, all of which lasted no longer than four months. If any of those jobs had worked out, The Sergei Foundation would have become a hobby, or maybe even disbanded. The hardships were all stepping stones. Once I finally decided to stop looking elsewhere and focus one hundred percent of my efforts on The Sergei Foundation, my true heart's desire to make a difference in the world, the trials stopped and miracles happened. My energy shifted, and that was recognized by donors. Yet again, another life lesson from Sergei.

I want to express a special thank you to Dr. Michael and Christine Morykwas whose belief in our mission and in my abilities gave The Sergei Foundation a solid foundation to build upon. Our good work continued, and The Sergei Foundation built up success stories and sustainability allowing us to be recipients of funding from grantors such as the Banfield Foundation, Petco Foundation, ASPCA and The Winston-Salem Foundation. I am so grateful for their support. Building on momentum, in 2014 I founded Triad Dog Games in Winston-Salem, NC. This event has grown to be one of the largest dog fundraising events in North Carolina, and so much fun! Even if you do not live in North Carolina, I encourage you to come and take part. You, your family, and your pet will have a blast.

The Sergei Foundation is still a small non-profit organization by most standards, yet we now assist over 100 dogs and cats yearly. We've granted more than $125,000 to date to help more than 800 people with financial assistance for veterinary medical services, referrals to other resources, free veterinary visit coupons, and more. That feels so good!

Our volunteer Board of Directors has a strategic plan with a goal of doubling those service numbers and charitable donations in the next four years so The Sergei Foundation can extend our program assistance to rescue or foster-based organizations. One step towards this goal is the creation of this book and sharing Sergei's and my stories. I hope that you will recommend *Sergei's Eyes* to others and buy copies to give as gifts, as all proceeds are donated directly to The Sergei Foundation.

Please visit SergeiFoundation.org to learn more. Read wonderful stories of the dogs and cats helped, and make a donation to help more pets like Jethro and Captain Marvel, who you will read about on the following pages.

Lastly, through Sergei's eyes, I have been able to see the world and myself differently. I feel I am more relaxed, more accepting, more loving. Pets teach us to give and to receive. They do not withhold their joy or excitement. They do not judge. They only offer love, play, and companionship. It is my wish that The Sergei Foundation continues to grow to serve more families and their beloved pets. I am grateful for all that has been accomplished so far, and I know we've only just begun.

Do you have a unique story or learning lesson from your pet? Please share them with me along with a photo of your cat or dog. Perhaps my next book will include the story of how your pet was your greatest teacher.

Email to: MyStory@KarenFullerton.com

Mail to:
The Sergei Foundation
My Pet Story
PO Box 17256
Winston-Salem, NC 27116

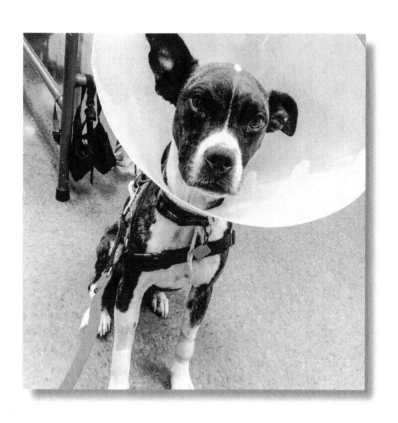

# *Jethro*

Jethro ate a rope toy and it extended throughout his intestines. The owner was at the emergency veterinary hospital crying and devastated because she could not afford the thousands of dollars they were quoting her. She believed she was going to have to say goodbye to her beloved pup.

The emergency clinic called The Sergei Foundation, and our network of veterinary partners provided Jethro a discounted price, enabling us to fund his life-saving surgery. It's not known exactly how long the rope had been ingested, but at the time of surgery the small intestines were black, had no blood supply, and ruptured in three places. After surgery, the veterinarian's prognosis was very guarded for survival; it was touch and go whether the intestines would start to function again. Thankfully, the surgery was a success and Jethro beat the odds! After a week, Jethro was able to go home. This time, his owner's tears were tears of joy. You can see a quick video of Jethro reuniting with his mom on the "In The News" link on SergeiFoundation.org.

# Captain Marvel

Meet Captain Marvel. She is a true super hero! At just two years old, veterinary care had an inconclusive diagnosis for the injury to her arm in the shoulder area. They thought she had been bitten by a poisonous spider. Not improving with medication, the veterinarian was now recommending amputation, a procedure the owner could not afford. That is when Captain Marvel's owner found The Sergei Foundation through a website search and applied for help.

The Sergei Foundation first assisted by obtaining a second veterinary opinion and diagnostic tests. Amputation is an invasive surgery and that route is taken only when absolutely necessary. After x-rays showed the bone was severely affected and porous, dangerously closing in on her neck, The Sergei Foundation was able to fund the amputation. Timing was very fortunate because if the bone decay had spread any further, even the amputation would not have been able to save this little girl's life. You can see Captain Marvel and her most grateful owners on a Fox8 News video on the "In The News" link on SergeiFoundation.org.

# Testimonials

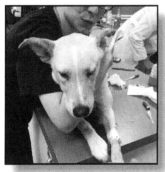

*Gracie Halfacre before surgery on her back leg.*

"My dog recently broke her leg. I was given three options, but the only financially possible route I had available to me was to put her down. I refused to let that happen, so I asked around and [applied to] The Sergei Foundation. They immediately contacted me with a life-saving grant and an excellent vet to perform the surgery. Gracie's now at home trying to eat my headphones again! Thank you to The Sergei Foundation for literally saving her life!"

Sheridan Halfacre
Roxboro, NC

*Blackie Connor
in her cast.*

"I am so appreciative of The Sergei Foundation's help. Of course for the financial to help with the amputation of our cat's leg, but the emotional support they gave me was worth so much to me. I'm not sure I would have made it through all of this without it."

Amber Connor
Greensboro, NC

*In loving memory of
Shea Bernat.*

"In working with Karen as she plans her annual Sergei Foundation fundraiser, the Triad Dog Games, it's apparent to me the passion Karen has for the welfare of animals and the strength she draws from her own personal experience."

Bonny Bernat
Manager, Visit Winston-Salem
Winston-Salem, NC

*In loving memory of Otis. Chad and Otis Tucker, June 10, 2016 during Otis' bucket list weekend.*

*"Over the years I've shared the stories of many families that have benefited from the resources of The Sergei Foundation. The greatest joy is personally meeting their beloved pets who are now living full and loved lives."*

Chad Tucker
Anchor/Reporter, Fox8 WGHP
High Point, NC